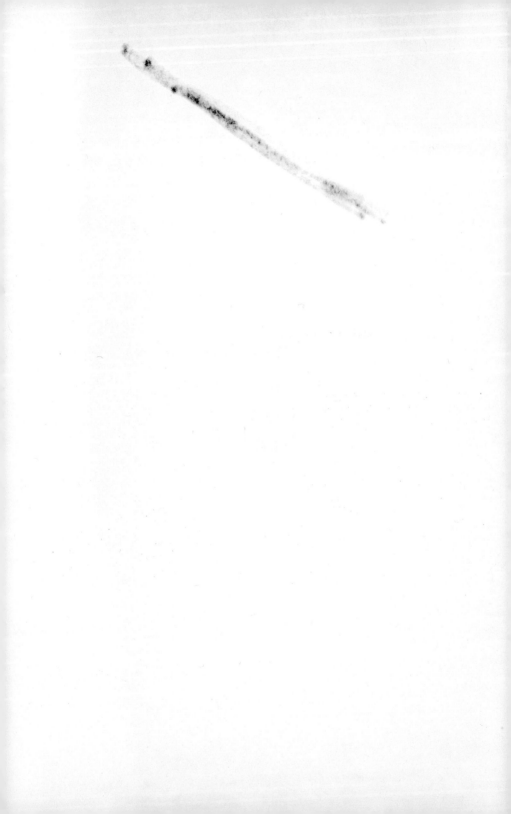

guide to the
disturbed
personality
through
handwriting

guide to the
disturbed personality through handwriting

Irene Marcuse, PH. D.

New York

Published by ARCO PUBLISHING COMPANY, Inc.
219 Park Avenue South, New York, N. Y. 10003
Copyright © Irene Marcuse, 1969
All Rights Reserved

Library of Congress Catalog Card Number 69-11206

Arco Book Number 668-01828-3

Printed in the United States of America

Foreword

OCCASIONALLY the right book appears at the right time to serve the right needs. Dr. Marcuse's *Guide to the Disturbed Personality Through Handwriting* is such a book.

Everywhere today, adults are struggling to achieve personal identity in a world in which events often defy rational solution. Indeed, the primary concern of people in the Space Age is not so much that of conquering new frontiers, as it is that of finding themselves in the most profound way.

Mothers and fathers without the answers can only raise children who are tragically lost. Quite rightly, today's thinking parents are asking such questions as: "How do I infuse a sense of personal values in my youngsters?" and "How, in a world of turmoil, do I communicate the supreme importance of inner harmony?"

Irene Marcuse offers in this book not theory, but practical solutions to these modern dilemmas. She concentrates on the central problems of our time. She begins at the beginning and shows how abnormalities in the child result in frustration. Then she traces, step by step, the demon of fear as it thwarts the healthy development of the child. She consistently approaches her subject from a positive point of view. You are shown how inhibition can be the source of neurosis and, how the scientific

5

principles of graphology can uncover danger signals in time for psychologists and other professionals to take corrective action before irreparable damage is done.

Dr. Marcuse makes a strong case for the fact that insufficient love is often the cause of mental illness. Self-love and self-respect, she says, must be learned before one can possibly hope to love others. Throughout the book the author gives many case studies and shows exactly what happened to real people with real-life problems. And she has included several samples of handwriting from the same individual's at progressive stages of mental deterioration.

Thus, in an aggressive, acquisitive society, this book offers the professional and layman alike a beacon of light. By intelligently combining the scientific principles of graphology with guidelines for achieving spiritual realization, Irene Marcuse has written a book of prime meaning for our time.

But, although the handwriting is a flawless mirror of mental dynamics, a study of this science cannot guarantee quick solutions. There are no panaceas. Certain individuals are beyond rehabilitation. But the mentally healthy and concerned individual will seek out the answers.

If you are searching for a practical means of understanding your problems and of dealing with them, this book is for you. You have only to use it and, then, go forth to light the world with the radiance of your deeper knowledge.

Paul M. von Freihofer

Acknowledgments

IT HAS ALWAYS been my desire to put together in a book my vast experiences in counseling people through analyses of their handwriting and in teaching the principles of graphology.

My friends and pupils have also long urged me to write a book, and some of them even provided me with samples of handwriting for the various chapters. I especially wish to thank Paul Goodman, John Melville, David Susskind, and Jean Kennedy.

The experience of putting the evidence together concerning the nature and meaning of handwriting analysis has proved extraordinarily exciting. Everything seemed to fall into place in a most enlightening way.

Contents

Introduction

FOR CENTURIES students of human nature have puzzled over the complex and difficult relationship between mind and body. No matter what their approach to man, most scientists have found it necessary to refer in some way to the unity of the human being. Yet, one of the most frustrating facts about this unity is that, when we focus on it, it seems to dissolve and slip from our grasp.

The following chapters show how, through graphology, we can gain new insight into this unity of body and mind. The psychological analysis of handwriting is invaluable for the purpose of exploring and describing personality.

The historical part of this science is discussed in my book *Guide to Personality Through Your Handwriting*,[1] which sets the stage for more thorough study of the uses of graphology in diagnosing mental problems. Thus, this second book is a natural development, relating in depth the science of handwriting to one of the most urgent problems of our day—mental disorder.

Educators, psychiatrists, and psychologists all over the country have long encouraged me to write this book. Indeed, there

---

[1] Published by Arc Books, Inc., New York.

is no other book on the market which successfully links handwriting analysis with the developing psyche.

What is the well-adjusted personality? What meaningful patterns can be detected in a child's handwriting? What are the danger signals? How does graphology reveal emotional disturbance in children and adults? These are among the questions discussed in this book. The basis of graphology is the assumption that we are what we write. Our handwriting explains what we are by revealing the way we have developed from child to adult.

This book is for everyone—laymen, counselors, and psychologists. The uses of graphology are many, for though the heart may lie, the handwriting never does!

1. How Abnormalities in the Growing Child Result in Frustration

No SINGLE individual can be viewed apart from the total setting in which he grows and lives. Thus, handwriting is important because it can give us insight into the background of the writer as well as into his present frustrations and abnormalities. In this chapter we shall study the incipient mental disorders, which, if detected in time, can be corrected before they become full-fledged mental diseases.

One should never overlook the cultural and psychological influence of the home or how it affects the social development of the individual. Very often, home and school are at the root of personality maladjustment. Young people's attitudes and characteristics are molded by all the conditions of their past and present lives—even by things that happened when they were infants.

The capacity to work with and become one of a group usually indicates a well-balanced personality. One who isolates himself is as disturbed as one who pursues association too urgently. Every healthy person in our culture strives to be well thought of and respected—the craving for acceptance is intuitive. However, one of the most common complaints made by the neurotic is that people dislike him, and this feeling usually manifests itself in profound maladjustment.

This sample of handwriting belongs to a fourteen-year-old girl who is very musical and has already given several successful public concerts. We see that the personal pronoun "I" is separated from the rest of the sentence, revealing her alienation from the rest of the family. Although the other words are written with more assurance, the continual change of slant shows her deep-seated tendency toward isolation.

At this stage of her development the child may not find it too difficult to master her sense of alienation and become more at ease with her surroundings. However, in order to make a healthy adjustment, she will need a great deal of help from those who are closest to her.

Interdependence is a basic law of life at every level. Individuation alone is not sufficient, though it is a necessary step. When the individual becomes truly adjusted to his environment, a growing sense of belonging will be found.

than that since I came home. Maybe we'll bring Essex to see you Wednesday, but then mightn't your mother object? Things are pretty solid now, I'm taking

This sample was written by a boy of fourteen whose parents are divorced. The wide spaces between words reveal his isolation, and the uneven basic line indicates his emotional instability. He is an intelligent child and is very eager to be one of the crowd, as is shown by the rightward slant and garlands. However, the uncertain strokes and the smeary pressure with which the boy writes clearly reveal the fact that he is maladjusted.

This boy's sense of identity suffers because he is insecure and lacks the feeling of belonging to a family group. His writing exhibits a downward trend, and the total effect indicates that he has little stamina or self-assurance.

Children who must live with unhappy or hostile parents will inevitably grow up with unnatural inhibitions—even when their parents have not been unreasonable in the restraints they have imposed and the punishments they have inflicted. Such physical inhibitions are often accompanied by emotional constriction and a decrease in intellectual growth. Frequently, such withdrawn individuals are torn between their impulses and their fears of expressing them, and this inner conflict can manifest itself in the form of neurosis.

This sample is the handwriting of a sixteen-year-old girl—an intelligent and gifted person who has already proven herself to be a talented actress and has great ambitions for a career on the stage. The loose and irregular script, in addition to the very light, uneven pressure, reveals her often confused and disorganized mind. She has been admitted to a mental hospital because of her frequent hallucinations and lack of coordination. Since she has no real consciousness of the difference between facts and her futile imaginings, she can never be relied on to tell the truth—she invents incidents at will. She also complains that people are trying to kill her. We see that the personal pronoun "I" is written totally without force, revealing her loss of identity. Because she became a drug addict in her early teens, she was unable to finish high school; however, she is drawn to the arts and shows rather good comprehension of the work of her favorite artists.

Many inhibited and maladjusted young people come from

Dear Miss Marcus:

I have never been as conscious of my handwriting as I am now. It is strange, yet exciting. I am most anxious

(See page 18)

families in which sibling antagonism is unusually intense. Having consistently failed to do as well as a particular brother or sister, a child may become resigned to failure. In so doing, he loses the ability to assert himself and eventually becomes unable to make any decisions. Fear of any and all competition makes him avoid situations in which effort or aggressiveness are required.

On page 17, the handwriting of an eighteen-year-old boy clearly reveals his mental and emotional problems. Most conspicuous is the fact that the personal pronoun "I" lies flat on its back, so to say, revealing that, despite his native intelligence and genuine will to accomplish, he lacks the strength of character needed to utilize his abilities with courage and enterprise. He is a pleasant, affectionate young man; however, the narrowness of the letters indicates that he suffers from fears which prevent him from expressing his most meaningful ideas and attitudes. On the other hand, the angularity of his letters suggests his ability to work well and his ambition to reach his goals. Fear is his obvious enemy—in spite of his abilities, he is afraid that, whatever he tries, others will outstrip him, and, thus, he feels it is useless even to try.

This otherwise-gifted young man needs psychiatric attention so that he can learn to recognize in himself the abilities and talents so obvious to other people. Without guidance, he may drift from one unimportant job to another, never taking advantage of his true potential.

Miss Irene Marcuse

243 West 100th St.

New York 25 N.Y.

Subsequently, at a later date, his handwriting shows that he is well on the way to self-realization. However, he still needs steady help if he is to overcome his lack of self-assurance completely. A person who feels that environmental pressures are too great and, as in the case of this young man, finds himself unable to deal with them usually adopts an attitude of impenetrability and aloofness and tries to remain emotionally frigid.

David, a boy of twelve, is adopted. He is the only child in the home of a well-to-do man in a small town. His parents are indulgent, and, being financially well off, they are able to give him many educational and social advantages. However, it was recommended that he undergo psychotherapy because of his constant stealing, both at home and elsewhere.

Because of his father's good social position in town, no one wanted to accuse the boy of being a thief. However, the fact that, over a period of months, he systematically stole things from several small department stores finally brought him to the attention of a social service agency. This agency discovered that, although it was true the boy had taken many things that did not belong to him, he usually returned the stolen objects within a day or two. It was also noted that he pretended to be afraid and was ill-at-ease with other children.

Studying the boy's handwriting (page 20) revealed that his relationship with his foster mother was not entirely felicitous. She overprotected him, terribly—possibly as a defense against any hostility she might secretly harbor toward him. However, the boy loved her, and his stealing was aimed at activating punishment, which he felt he deserved. Since this punishment was not forthcoming he decided to run away. In his resentment and by running away, he was expressing his unconscious hope of finding his real parents. The narrowness of his letters, in addition to the wiry pressure he exerts, indicates a strong, neurotic personality.

Dear Tommy:

I think this week went slow. My favorite subject is Health.

Someday I hope to be a doctor.

(See page 19)

Summary

In this chapter we have demonstrated the extreme importance of examining the individual only in the context of his total environment. Specific examples of persons who failed to adjust successfully were discussed along with samples of their handwriting. Graphological evidence supports the following conclusions:

1. The well-balanced personality relates well to his group.
2. Individuation in itself is not enough; it must be accompanied by interdependence.
3. Inhibition of the youth's spontaneity is often the source of neurosis. Definite clues in the handwriting can reveal this problem.
4. Sibling antagonism often results in personality blockage.

2. The Results of Fear in the Growing Child

YOUNG PEOPLE often develop strong feelings of antagonism and hostility toward adults who refuse to let them make their own decisions.

This twenty-year-old girl's handwriting is that of an over-protected only child. She was described by her mother as having been exceedingly aggressive at home but withdrawn when she first entered school. Unless urged, she did not participate in play programs or work with children in the classroom, and she always feigned physical illness to avoid going to school or summer camp.

Her mother said she was extremely orderly, a behavior pattern which she had imposed on the child. The mother had often beaten her child; and, by the time the girl was six, she had begun to show several abnormal fears. After viewing television, she had nightmares and complained of witches in her bed. She was also afraid of a dog which she had to pass on her way to school.

By the time she wrote the above letter at the age of twenty, she was addicted to drugs and had been committed to a mental hospital. That she was very intelligent, even artistic and creative, is revealed by her original letter formations. However, the light-pressured and loose script, in addition to the ever-changing slant, shows the inconsistency of her personality. She clearly was mentally disturbed. Her exaggerated sexual desire, which remained unfulfilled, is shown by the inflated lower loops, some turned back to self. Since she had neither physical nor mental resilience, no one was ever able to help her, and she eventually committed suicide.

The psychopathic personality is a special form of character disorder in which the superego is seriously defective or non-existent. These patients are so devoid of regulative principles that they are often regarded as mere imbeciles, and they frequently suffer from organic deficiencies.

Any attempt to define psychopathy is necessarily complicated by the fact that constitutional factors and organic inferiorities play an important part in determining social adjustments. There are, however, certain definite characteristics which almost invariably indicate a psychopathic personality. In order to determine whether or not a patient is a psychopath, we must observe the way in which he deals with interpersonal relationships and social situations as well as the way in which he accepts or rejects the moral demands of everyday life. The true psychopath is evasive; yet, on the other hand, he often possesses a disarming kind of charm that deceives many people. In his handwriting this is shown by the fact that his letters are large, written with heavy pressure, and contain many futile flourishes. One of the chief characteristics of a psychopath is that he lacks moral judgment and tends to disregard social mores, rules, and regulations. Other characteristics are selfishness and inability to form meaningful relationships. Most of his friendships are perfunctory and superficial, established for his own personal advantage, rather than out of any affection for the other party.

On page 26 is a sample of the script of a man of thirty. Notice the futile flourishes and large, angular letters with blown-up and angular lower loops. These indicate evasiveness and dishonesty, two of the most common evidences of the psychopathic personality.

The handwriting belongs to an intelligent and well educated man, who possesses good mental abilities and logical thought processes. This is indicated by the fact that the letters are well formed with even spacing between words and lines, in addition to a good form level. The writer is easily capable of fulfilling his obligations, and he really tries to utilize his genuine mental capabilities. However, we notice that the tempo of his writing is erratic. He is cantankerous, always blaming others for his own failures. Although he can be a good social mixer, his unfortunate thoughts of the past have negatively influenced his whole outlook on life and have disturbed him to such an extent that even his physical condition suffers. He complains of many ailments, is steadily under a physician's care, and, in spite of his talents, is unable to live a normal and constructive life.

Psychotherapy deals largely with the interpersonal relationships of people who are maladjusted due to the fact that their normal, orderly growth has been interfered with and inhibited. Psychotherapy attempts to strengthen these people's egos and the 4th [firamann?] —

would July. As you will remember —

reference Esther is the important member

[careful delegation?].

The host of each of general and diverse —

our [?] you [?] server of that is the

[?] our writer of the family. Our

the next of the tribe.

requested, requesting proof of delivery. This procedure should make us all style conscious of the use of embroidery for desirable or captivating effects that help sell garments whether they sold in New York or live in Mexico - did Both and Jerry when they get back will fill in many other details and only the future can prove the Romano Brothers' integrity or honest dealings with us concerning Adonna.

(See page 28)

to improve their self-images. Overt and covert anxieties must be dealt with, and it is always necessary to ascertain the sources of these fears and frustrations.

The handwriting on page 27 belongs to a man of forty-five, and it shows typical psychoneurotic characteristics. The presence of anxiety is readily discernible in the wiry, narrow, unsure script; and the futile flourishes adorning the letters reveal both the writer's anxiety and his distortion of reality. In such an anxious state he cannot perceive reality clearly. On the contrary, he sees it either as a threat or as an object of hostility. This writer denies painful truths and escapes into a world of hallucination and delusion. As with all psychoneurotics, his inability to face reality is the result of conflict between his id and superego.

Acting-out and destructiveness are parts of the total psychoneurotic personality. The script on page 29 shows at a glance a marked behavioral disorder. As a child he displayed a neurotic character and usually became intensely disturbed when his hyperactivity was impeded or when he was disciplined.

Even when fear made him less aggressive for a brief period, the inner pressures manifested themselves in restlessness. He was never able to play quietly, despite his best intentions. At present, this thirty-two-year-old man's behavior picture shows clearly in his handwriting. However, the forces and impulses which resulted in this behavior are extremely complex.

Ambivalence is a state of struggle and indecision which causes emotional and physical debility due to the fact that, whenever a decision has to be made, an exorbitant amount of energy is wasted in the resolution of conflict.

Psychotherapy seeks to remove this indecision by helping the patient develop emotional clarity and become a more decisive individual. It seeks to destroy his old uncertainty and oscillation. When a patient is able to bring forward his repressed, negative, guilt-evoking impulses and fantasies and to recognize and accept them, his conflict can be reduced or eliminated.

handle it. I'm sure you could do it on $200 total. It seems if you quit drinking and eating for a couple of months you could handle it. We don't have to leave dept. (≠ you know you could work through until you had enough. If you landed a good job, you could make $900 ~ two summer easily. If we got a good

(See page 28)

From this sample of his handwriting, it is apparent that the subject has not, as yet, established a desirable balance between his conflicting impulses. However, he has learned to act decisively and unfalteringly. Although conflict has been reduced somewhat through increased understanding, prolonged treatment will be necessary in order to make this intelligent and capable man function cooperatively.

Behold & see as you pass by,
As you are now
So once was I
As I am now
You soon will be
Prepair for death
And follow me.

This sixteen-year-old boy's handwriting shows that he has high native intelligence. The original way in which he shapes his letters reveals that he is also, at least to some extent, a creative and imaginative person. However, his loose script, written with very light pressure, indicates his rather unsure, infantile personality and his deep-seated feelings of weakness. To those who know him, his gait and bodily movements give the impression of poor muscle coordination.

A complete neurological examination indicated that, in spite of his intelligence, the boy displayed poor perception. The test also showed that much of his passivity was the result of his lack of an authority figure, such as a strong mother or father, with whom he could identify. His waking fantasies and dreams revealed an inhibited, fearful young man, who saw the world as a threat. This young man grew up; he developed his native intelligence. However, his basic mental condition continued to deteriorate, and eventually he lost all sense of identity.

The above sample was written by the same boy when he was twenty-five. We see remnants of the boy of sixteen in his script; for example, the personal pronoun "I" is almost the same. However, we realize his complete confusion. He knows several languages and can converse quite intelligently at times, but, as this script clearly shows, he has completely lost his sense of identity and his reasoning powers.

Summary

The purpose of this chapter was to show the way in which fear prevents the growing child from making a successful adjustment to life. The following points were made:

1. Overprotection of the child can result in adverse psychological traits. Light pressured, loose script and ever-changing slant are the graphological clues.

2. The superego is either weak or non-existent in the psychopathic personality.

3. The characteristics of the psychopathic personality are amorality, evasiveness, and acceptive charm. His handwriting shows <u>futile flourishes</u> and <u>erratic</u> movement.

4. Acting and destructiveness are parts of the total personality of the psychoneurotic. He is unable to strike a balance between his comflicting impulses. Psychotherapy attempts to help the patient identify his fear-evoking impulses and fantasies for purposes of self-recognition and elimination.

3. Fear: The Destructive Force in the Personality

PERSONALITY IS an achievement and not simply a datum of genetics. To be oneself, to comprehend one's own personality to the fullest extent is mankind's greatest goal.

A man who is free from fear is said to have an integrated, individuated, or whole personality. Fear can exert a lethal influence. The remedy for fear is consciousness of freedom, a faith in God, and that requires insight—a somewhat ambiguous term that has been incorporated into psychiatric terminology. Although the concept of insight is often confused with the concept of understanding, insight actually refers to a rather emotional accommodation and flexibility within the person's psyche that transcends intellectual understanding.

The script on page 34 belongs to a woman of thirty-eight, who was reared in a broken home. Many circumstances combined to interfere with her natural growing-up processes. She was, however, a good student in school, afraid always that her grades were below what her mother expected of her. She lived in an environment of total misunderstanding between herself and her mother. We can perceive from her script's light, uneven pressure

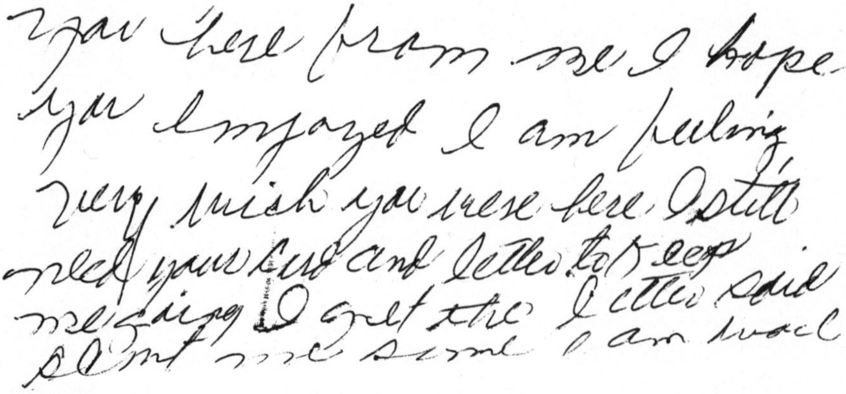

[handwritten text]

and loose, large letter formations that she is now completely beyond any rational concept of herself or those around her. Steady hallucinations darken her self-conception. Although she occasionally has moments of relative rationality and can sometimes converse with logic and intelligence, she is not ready yet to rely entirely on herself. Therefore, she still needs the protection of the mental hospital.

A state of fear always leads to further reactions, such as flight, submission, or attack.

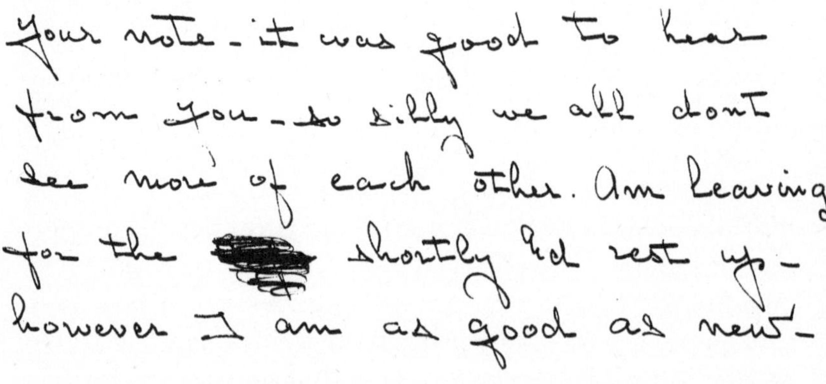

[handwritten text]

This sample was written by a thirty-year-old man, who is a homosexual. According to his case history, he became a homosexual because his fear of rejection and injury in love made it impossible for him to obtain or give normal, heterosexual love. However, his homosexuality lowers his self-esteem, not only because of cultural mores, but also because the very act seems humiliating to him. In addition, he is constantly expecting some catastrophe to befall him. The writer was, at one time, a school teacher; his keen intelligence and excellent education are revealed by the even spacing between words and lines and by the good "form level"—i.e., the high degree of aesthetic balance and the originality of the form of the sample. He was particularly interested in teaching retarded children and felt qualified to give them special attention. However, the warm pressure with which he makes his horizontal lines and the wideness of his spacing reveals his abnormality.

He is a warmhearted person who wanted a mission in life, and he was a success in his work. Not surprisingly, he had a special regard for boys, and, despite his fine personality and dedication to his job, he could not sublimate his homosexuality. Once this was discovered, he was dismissed from his position. The incident affected his mind to such a degree that it was necessary to commit him to a mental hospital.

Before we discuss our next case, let us look for a moment at graphological personality tests, in addition to others such as the Wechsler and Szondi. The Rorschach Test is not a personality test per se, since it is used mainly to determine emotional stability. In such tests as the Wechsler and Szondi the examiner needs to be able to observe or talk to the testee; however, this is not necessary in handwriting analysis. In a graphological test the person being analyzed is asked only to write, in his accustomed way, anything he desires, preferably using pen and ink. He should write enough to cover a page or slightly less and should give his age and sex.

This sample is inspected as a whole to determine the form level—an examination which requires a considerable degree of experience and judgment on the part of the examiner. After the form level has been determined, the sample is analyzed for various characteristics. In interpreting these traits, we must consider them, not separately, but in light of the form level as well as in relation to the other characteristics exhibited in the handwriting. For example, speed of writing may be interpreted as "agility" in one case and as "haste" in another. If the form level is poor, one is inclined to interpret it as haste.[1]

This is the handwriting of a nineteen-year-old boy who had chronic difficulty in concentrating. Otherwise, he was a bright boy, a good student who showed keen perception and even great versatility and flexibility in the way he treated his subjects. His lack of concentration, however, prevented him from taking advantage of his many mental endowments.

His vivid imagination, which led him to invent stories, was admired by all the students of his class, and he was happy being the center of attention.

As we can see from his confused script, with its continual change of slant, poor spacing, and extreme irregularity, this otherwise gifted person will not succeed in his endeavors until he overcomes his mental and emotional problems. Because of his inability to concentrate, he failed examinations; and, as a consequence, he was punished at home for his laziness.

---

[1] Marcuse, Irene, *Guide to Personality Through Your Handwriting* (ARC Books, Inc., New York, 1965).

His handwriting clearly indicates his mental condition; how-ever, it also shows the writer's courage, and the sharp and trian-gular lower loops even give evidence of a certain pugnacity. The whole script depicts his great imaginative power, which, unfortunately, was misdirected.

This young man's history reveals that no one recognized his chronic state of anxiety because he always tried to conceal it with boisterous behavior, the better to appear courageous. As we can detect from this script, the writer is basically an intro-vert. This is shown by the tightly closed vowels and the fact that the letters are narrow in comparison to their size. Conversely, he gives the impression of being an extrovert.

This boy did not receive sufficient love as a child. He felt rejected. His mother was not affectionate; yet, she was over-protective. She was emotionally distant, still oversolicitous and overbearing in her discipline. The father, who was loving, died when his son was very young. The boy felt both dominated and rejected. The loss of his father deprived him of the only source of affection which was in any way equivalent to his needs.

It is axiomatic that children who are denied love usually grow up to be what we call "insecure personalities." This young man was always afraid; he lived only for appearances, while his inner self remained empty. As a boy, he was resentful and hostile toward the uncooperative, threatening, punishing, frustrated adult.

His resentment resulted from the fact that he felt he was unfairly treated. He became hostile to those individuals on whom he depended and whom he needed to love. Being stronger than he, however, they formulated his goals and ideals for him. This, in turn, led to a great fear of abandonment and complete frustration of his bodily wants.

His steady fear, in addition to his feelings of helplessness, eventually contributed to a catastrophic breakdown.

Summary

Fear, the destructive force in the personality, is a result of the individual's thwarted development between childhoood and maturity. The evolution of fear has been demonstrated by several case studies. The following conclusions were made:

1. The ideal remedy for fear is consciousness of freedom, which requires the development of insight.

2. Observable broad patterns and responses reveal the integrated features in the patient's total behavior.

3. Inadequate love is often the basic cause of subsequent mental disintegration.

4. The form level refers to the combination of aesthetic balance and originality in the person's writing. This is the central feature in handwriting analysis.

5. Specific handwriting traits offer clues which can prevent difficulty if correctly interpreted in time.

4. How A Lack of Faith in Ourselves Leads to Frustration and Aggression

To MANY PEOPLE the true test of maturity is the ability to have satisfactory relations with the opposite sex; to others it is the ability to be at one with society; still others feel that to be individuated is paramount. All these are, in truth, a means of expressing the same essential condition.

The final achievement, which is self-realization or recognition of one's singular personality, is the fullest possible expression in life of the innate potentialities of the individual. Everyone, conciously or unconciously, is seeking a certain goal. However, men vary in numerous ways—in intelligence, physique, temperament, and so forth. By no means is it implied that any man should strive after a goal beyond his individual capacity. If we learn to recognize our own abilities and limitations, we are all capable of attaining a certain harmony, an inner wholeness, and a satisfactory relationship between our work and the world. This is as true of the less gifted person as it is of the highly gifted one.

It is the graphologist's task to aid his client in realizing himself more fully. Whatever method the graphologist employs,

I just got back from Steve's Apartment. He told me all about Europe I really sounds cool. Talk to your other ladies and give my to the world. Be you gotta

(See page 41)

his basic aim is to help another person live his life more completely. However, the handwriting expert must be careful not to attempt to influence the external events and circumstances of his client's life or to attempt to convert him to the graphologist's frame of reference or philosophy.

Let us begin with the handwriting (page 40) of a young man of twenty. He is rich with original ideas. Specifically, he is a painter who also sculpts.

From his original letter formations we learn that this young man has talent and artistic imagination. He works fast, and ideas come easily to him. On the other hand, even as he never completes his letters but allows them to spread in different directions, he also begins his artistic work with great enthusiasm but tires of it easily. He begins many works simultaneously, is very impatient, and never completes anything. His case history shows that, because of his inability to finish his projects, he finally lost his confidence in ever being able to accomplish anything worthwhile. He changed locales often, thinking that in Europe he would find more understanding. Unfortunately, the same thing happened in Europe that had happened in the United States. He became listless and, finally, lost all faith in himself. In a state of overpowering depression he committed suicide.

Frustration results when our desires remain unfilled. When certain basic desires are not satisfied, the personality, particularly the self-esteem or feeling of security is threatened, as in the case of this young artist.

The writer of the sample on page 42 is a man of twenty-five. From the many flourishes of his handwriting we can gather that he has a higher opinion of himself and his accomplishments than is justified. The stilted capitals and ornate script reveal a person who is convinced that he knows everything better than others.

On the other hand, he is not really as sure of himself as he

Hampton - Maccar Institution August 1, 1966

Please send me information regarding your correspondent course.

Thank you

(See page 41)

pretends to be. The hidden change of slant signifies his self-doubt. His vanity, however, is all too genuine.

We must realize that every conflict in a person is accompanied by a persistent, though perhaps unconsious, effort toward its resolution. Conflicts are painful for several obvious reasons. They destroy the individual's sense of integration and organization, and they lead to a feeling of indecision. This can present a threat to one's self-esteem.

For example, this young man finally realized that it was useless to pretend, and he lost his imaginary self-confidence. This, however, did not solve his problem. A self-examination caused deep depression. Luckily a psychiatrist was eventually able to help him overcome his problems.

If confusion is to be avoided, we must distinguish between the concepts of deprivation and frustration. Frustration results from deprivation. From the above case we can see that non-gratification of desires can be a threat to the personality. This young man's frustration was circumvented by intelligent psychiatric counseling, which he accepted, thus pointing his way toward success in life.

Aggression is one of the most universal and serious effects of frustration. The strength of the tendency to aggression depends on the amount of frustration.

Aggression may be direct or indirect. In its simplest and strongest form it is merely aimed at the person who is causing the frustration. If this direct aggression is blocked for some reason, an indirect or substitute form may be expected.

Page 44 shows the writing of a woman of fifty-five. The large, angular letters reveal the writer's desire to be seen and heard. However, the fact that the personal pronoun "I" is lying flat on its back reveals that the writer's desire remains unfulfilled. This is true because of her rebellious and overly critical nature, and the frustration of her desire has made her very aggressive. There are different forms of aggression; thus, instead of punching someone, this woman started rumors in an attempt to hurt

I am interested in hand-
writing analysis not as a
hobby but as a vocation.
If I studied and learned
how could I apply it so
that I might be able to
make an intellectual income
out of it - what fields would
be open for one, who too for

(See page 43)

certain people whom she suspected of being unfriendly toward her.

She is convinced that she is superior to others, and this self-evaluation is revealed in her very large script with its poor spacing.

She wants to study graphology, but this has to be discouraged because of her lack of self-knowledge and consequent failure to understand human nature. However, she is a tenacious person and is not likely to give up her goal easily.

She feels strong hostility, which may be expressed in an excessively violent way, such as a temper tantrum. Because of her pronounced insistence on asserting herself without accepting instruction, she could never be a good student. Since she is already fifty-five, it seems improbable that she will be able to benefit from the study of graphology or to apply any acquired knowledge successfully.

Summary

In this chapter we have taken a realistic look at frustration and fear. In case after case we have seen that the major cause of frustration and fear is the absence of a well developed sense of self-esteem. The following conclusions result:

1. Self-realization is a universal goal. The potential for internal harmony or wholeness exists in everyone.

2. When the personality is threatened, one is usually unable to develop self-confidence.

3. Every conflict in the individual bears the seed of resolution.

4. Lack of successful personality integration is the result of non-gratification of desire, frustration, or both.

5. Aggression is one of the most universal and serious effects of frustration. It may be expressed directly or indirectly.

5. How Inhibition Limits the Capacity to Love

PEOPLE'S ATTITUDES toward sex play a vital role in the development of their personalities. No matter what an individual's emotional attitudes may be, he cannot prevent sex from exerting a vital influence over his daily thoughts and actions. No matter how hard one tries to avoid the thought of sex, it cannot be divorced from one's life. It can be ignored, and it can be made distasteful; however, none of these reactions minimizes its importance. Sex is too determined a biological reality to be excised from life.

It is futile to try to deal with the sexual aspects of one's personality by simply denying their existence; any attitude other than an inquiring and positive one is self-defeating. In recent years we have come to treat sex with greater respect because we have begun to realize the influence it exerts over other aspects of our personality and the ways in which the experiences of childhood and youth color our sexual attitudes. Psychiatrists, of whatever persuasion, have long been convinced of the inescapable importance of sex in every adult situation. Sex very literally aspires to be our friend or enemy, for it either helps or hinders our adjustment to every situation.

People in love want much more than physical satisfaction. Most people also attribute tremendous importance to such things as compassion, understanding, respect, and the ability to communicate with another person. Naturally, the inability to analyze and refine sexual experience accounts for many of the maladjustments that occur between men and women; however, it is a mistake to say that sex has come to count for too much in our society. Ignorance, confusion, and guilt about sex are slowly disappearing and are being replaced by mature, deepened, and educated attitudes.

It is axiomatic that success in life is achieved most effectively with a maximum of self-knowledge and understanding and a minimum of the shallow emulation of others. Striving "to be someone else" is inviting failure. Similarly, the person who is confined by a rigid set of rules and expected to grow up to fit a certain mold suffers accordingly, as is apparent in the following example of the script of an eighteen-year-old girl.

Reared in a strict small town environment (her father held a minor executive position), this girl was constantly reminded that she must always strive for blameless behavior, not for reasons of morality, but because anything else would threaten her parents' social position.

The parents were strict in their religious observance, and the children (the subject had a younger brother) were required to attend church functions. On the face of it, they were a close-knit family with traditional, not to say exaggerated, middle-class attitudes. They operated, self-consciously, within a very carefully budgeted, modest income. See page 49 for a sample of her handwriting.

The girl was an excellent musician with a lovely voice and was very active in church choir. In her day-to-day relationships she could be pronouncedly stubborn and even alarmingly temperamental. In her script this is shown by the long, angular lower extensions in addition to outsized capitals.

As a rule, she was poised and a model of exemplary be-

This teaching will be on a part time basis — probably two full days a week. At M.H. Tch piano is a required part of the curriculum for music majors. Therefore, the course carries a credit and I will be grading each student. The master class plan will be in effect, with Mr. Istomin coaching the girls in groups of two and three after I have done the groundwork, so to speak. The college is

(See page 48)

havior. She earned the respect of her classmates while maintaining a fine scholastic record. The fact remains, all too evidently, that this extremely regulated upbringing and the severe checks it placed on any excessive or unprescribed behavior were utterly at odds with her basic temperament. The overlong extensions in a narrow script show that she was basically sanguine and more than a little outgoing. However, she was denied any expression of the sexual desires that are natural to a girl her age.

When circumstances placed her on her own, she turned her back on her past with its strictures and harsh admonitions. In the confusion of her new unfettered existence, she ran off with the first boy who aided her in rebellion. As might be imagined, he eventually deserted her, and, fearing beyond anything a return home and censure, she became more and more desperate and finally took her own life.

The psychologist W. W. Boehm once wrote, "Mental health is a condition and level of social functioning, which is acceptable socially and personally satisfying."[1] People, then, are happiest when they know that what life offers them corresponds closely with what they truly want. If an individual can extract real happiness and a sense of well-being from the world as he knows it, then, whatever his merits, he can be considered mentally healthy.

The handwriting on page 51 is that of a twenty-eight year old man. He is, according to his friends, a happy person, enterprising and enthusiastic. He has fashioned his world with himself at its center, and he refuses to let anything interfere with his own happiness. He enjoys addressing assemblies, the larger and more enthusiastic the better, and he knows how to lay just the right stress on interest and entertainment.

While he can often be convincing and even logical (note the even spacing between words), his mind is hopelessly disorganized, and he is unable to complete most of the ambitious projects

---

[1] *Mental Health and Mental Disorder*, W. W. Norton, 1955.

(See page 50)

he starts. In his personal dealings he betrays the profound egocentricity of his nature. His friendships are important to him only inasmuch as they are useful and serve to burnish his glowing reputation. Given a premise, any premise, he will immediately bring the subject back to himself. The personal pronoun "I" is obviously conspicuous in this example. In fact, it dominates everything he writes.

His complete absorption in his own well-being extends to his marriage. His sexual appetites are pronounced, and he frequently makes excessive demands on his wife with no thought to her pleasure or feelings. He is promiscuous and likes to believe he is favoring women with his attention. The exaggerated personal pronoun, closed in on itself, gives away these traits.

A sense of proportion and of the rightness of things is invaluable in this life, and an absence of these qualities is easily discerned in handwriting. In his book, *Man Against Himself*,[2] Dr. Karl Menninger says:

> Let us define health as the adjustment of human beings to the world and to each other with a maximum of effectiveness and happiness. Not just efficiency, or just contentment—or the grace of obeying the rules of the game cheerfully. It is all of these together. It is the ability to maintain an even temper, an alert intelligence, socially considerate behavior and a happy disposition. This, I think is a healthy mind.

The example which follows was written by a man, sixty-nine, born in Germany and now a resident of the United States. He is a doctor with a long career marked by solid accomplishments and unflagging devotion. His many friends describe him as loyal and affable, possessed of an unusually perceptive sense of humor in all things.

What his friends might not be in a position to recognize, or could discount too readily, is his disproportionate and too quickly triggered enthusiasm. This is shown by the long strokes

---

[2] Published by Harcourt, Brace & World, Inc., New York.

Enclosed find your receipt from Hotel Rizzo, which you may need for Internal Revenue Service.

It was good to talk to you, give my regards to your family from house to house

over the letters and the extended initial strokes. This enthusiasm makes him too ready to espouse new and untested theories. It is merely lucky that this tendency has not interfered with his work; it has proven disastrous in his private life.

When he met the woman he was to marry, he had been a bachelor for many years. All the exaggerated enthusiasm he had hitherto reserved for his work was channeled suddenly into winning the hand of this girl, who was much younger than he. His better judgment and the natural precautionary advice of his close friends availed not at all in the face of the chronic over-exuberance that characterized his behavior. The young lady was understandably impressed by his avid courtship and imposing achievements; they were married in a matter of weeks.

Only the subject could tell what he had imagined the marriage would be. One might suppose that the girl would have had to be something more than human to even begin to match his shattering anticipation. In the awkwardness of the circumstances they proved to be incompatible. It is interesting to note that

I enjoy hearing from people in
Duluth from time to time. I expect
that I must write a letter in order
to justify an expectation of a return.
So I will be writing to various
people from time to time.

(See page 55)

the subject brought to the mechanics of the divorce the same over-riding enthusiasm he had always exhibited.

The sample on page 54 is from a man of thirty-six who has many talents. He is a capable attorney and is quite well known in his field. With equal success he could have pursued any of the sciences, politics, or the humanities. The form level of his handwriting is excellent.

In spite of all this, he is lacking in emotional maturity. He has been engaged several times and has weathered two notably unsuccessful marriages. The very clarity and decisiveness that mark his work are markedly absent from his personal life. He is not friendly, and what little leisure his schedule allows him is squandered aimlessly. Note that in his handwriting the line direction is wavering and there is rhythmical disturbance; freedom of movement is lacking and there is a general want of integration.

There is speed exhibited in this script, though it is spasmodic. It appears on the face of it to be well-proportioned. Still, there are disturbing fluctuations of an abruptness that indicates a basic underlying conflict of direction and an inconsistency in pursuit of his goals.

Summary

This chapter has attempted analysis of those people who are unable to express their feelings clearly. It appears that many thousands of troubled people of all sorts seek fulfillment, but they are affected by emotional states which prevent them from fully utilizing their mental and physical endowments.

6. How to Establish Harmony Between Personal Life and Work

IF THERE COULD be said to be one set of characteristics by which we measure a person's degree of adjustment, they would be the following: his ability to love; his adequacy in love, work, and play; his adequacy in interpersonal relations; his expediency in the solutions of problems. A person's ability to establish harmony between his personal life and work, to keep one from conflicting with the other, is one important sign that he is well adjusted.

For example, a man may be ambitious, devoted to his work, successful, and well respected in his profession. On the other hand, as a husband and father he may be less successful. Whenever work and family life conflict, he characteristically decides in favor of work. If judged by his ability to love, work, and play, he would be found lacking in mental health.

The foundations of mental health are self-acceptance, self-confidence, and self-reliance. Self-acceptance suggests that a person has learned to live with himself; self-confidence and self-reliance show that a person has gained self-respect. However, in applying these and other standards, it is important to remember that we are, more often than not, too quick to label

(See page 59)

people normal or abnormal. We often regard only those people who share our ideas as sensible. Mental health is relative after all.

Many people exhibit an excess of energy to harness their feelings or to mask their emotions to the extent that they become emotionally impoverished. The script on page 58 is a case in point. The writer is a man of forty-two. His narrow, very angular and small letters reveal his emotional impoverishment.

From the good form level we gather that the writer is a highly educated and intelligent person, independent in his thoughts and actions. He was not, in fact, born left-handed, but he acquired the ability to write with his left hand because, as a result of polio in his early years, he has only partial use of his right arm and hand. In spite of this handicap, he writes fluently with good speed.

The long upper and lower loops on his letters show his enthusiastic personality, and the well developed script shows his heightened perception of literature and the arts. The strict regularity reveals his fine and exacting working habits. Such a man would seem bound to make a success of any career to which he devotes his talent and energy. However, his inability to express himself emotionally—his basic incapacity for operating on an adult level—means that, although eventual success always lies within his grasp, its achievement will be hard won.

At first sight, one is impressed with the particular originality and the superior form level of the writing on page 60. These, together with the speed of the movements and simplifications of letters indicate the great intelligence of Paul Goodman. His writing clearly expresses a sense of logical and qualitative discrimination, and this shows Dr. Goodman's ability to perceive essentials readily. The handwriting is markedly rhythmical and well-integrated. This holds true for the degree of connectedness.

On the one hand, the falling endings indicate depression, and, on the other, the often dashing t-bars reveal enthusiasm. Dr. Goodman can also assert himself obstinately, not caring whether

Dear Irene,

The enclosed is a specimen of actual composition. I write in pencil on 8½ x 11 sheet. You ask me to include an l, and I seem to vary between I and l. I used to write a bit smaller. Send me the fruits of your research. Us.

(See page 59)

he loses or gains friends. He can be a stickler for details, and, at the same time, strikingly original in his thoughts. This is surely a rare combination!

Paul Goodman's sense of humor, revealed by the wavy t-bars, is most refreshing. The letters have a quality of both quiet determination and restrained imagination. His emotional life is somewhat misdirected—the letters lack regularity and persistent connectedness.

The whole script demonstrates that the writer has had since childhood free, imaginative access to his psychic resources. This makes him a warm and effortless observer of human nature.

The heavy, even pressure and the clear, well-sized, original formation of letters in David Susskind's script on page 62 reveal at once a man with dominant leadership qualities. The excellent form level shows his creative, independent thought processes.

The dynamic force of his handwriting discloses that he is an individualist, independent, efficient, and purposeful. He is extremely ambitious, and this, together with his great desire to succeed, allows him to stubbornly pursue his goals to their logical ends. Obstacles are to him a challenge, rather than a handicap.

The heavy, even, and warm pressure testifies that this writer is a warm-hearted person, one who can be affectionate and loving in his personal life and yet pursue a brilliant career. As a consequence, he is admired for his integrity and liked for his warmth and his sympathetic understanding, both in his private and professional lives.

Miss Jean Kennedy displays in her script (on page 63), with its heavy, even pressure and original letter formations, a woman of high intelligence augmented by an excellent educational background.

She is a capable organizer and will accomplish her tasks in her own original manner with real efficiency. The even size of her large and regular letters indicates her personal integrity.

(See page 61)

(See page 61)

Friday April 29, 1966

Dear Mrs. Harcourt —

I should always type my letters, as friends tell me they have a difficult time reading my handwriting. When I'm careful and write slowly - it's more legible !

She is sound of mind and body, emotionally and mentally stable, and, in addition, a kind and affectionate person.

Her universe is full of quiet courage. Gifted with good judgment of people and situations, she is always courteous and sensitive toward others. This lady certainly is capable of maintaining a good balance between her professional and personal lives.

Summary

We have tried to demonstrate by means of handwriting analysis that how well a person fits into the particular niche he has selected for himself is not as significant as how effectively he is able to adapt to the exigencies of the moment and how much he can mold his environment to fit the needs of his personality.

A person who loves his work and is capable of combining it with his love for and responsibility to his family surely must be called a well-rounded individual.

7. How Handwriting Gives Clues to Mental Illness

WHEN PEOPLE are unable to control their emotions, when they are prone to temper tantrums or crying spells, we are quick to say that they have emotional problems. Often we do not realize that the opposite tendencies, such as increasing calm and marked passivity, can also indicate mental illness.

When a person does not express his emotions, we tend to regard it as part of his normal character development, rather than as a warning that he may be headed toward mental illness. To many people the expression of emotion while they were growing up brought pain. To escape this pain these people learned to ignore their feelings. They became afraid to acknowledge that they had any emotions at all. But they end up paying too high a price for their comfort—they become emotionally impoverished. Thus, they stifle their capacity for living fully and richly.

In order to understand an individual's present attitudes, we must go back to his early childhood and see how he learned to express or control his feelings. The past always sheds its light on what we are now. (See page 66 for a sample of his handwriting.)

with their mouths hanging down)
that rainwater into the cistern);
and on the window ledge, at every
floor, in a pot of painted earthenware,
a basil or heliotrope blossomed.

Gustave Flaubert:
Legend of St. Julian the
Hospitaler

(See page 65)

By the time he was twenty-three, Gustave Flaubert had finished his education and become a teacher of French at the high-school level. He was intellectually mature and knew how to utilize his talents. His emotional maturity, however, lagged far behind his mental development. He was the typical neurotic, completely involved in himself.

We observe that his vowels are tightly closed and written with unsure strokes; some letters look as if they have been retraced. The rhythmical qualities of the script show that this man is so moody that it actually affects his movements and changes his characteristic gestures. The extreme slowness in the handwriting of so well educated a man indicates that he suffers periods of deep depression.

Flaubert was extremely introverted—so introverted, in fact, that he was unaware that the children he was teaching were uncomfortable with him and made fun of him. Thus, in spite of his mental acumen, his superiors decided that he was incompetent and dismissed him from his position.

Identification on my part may be evident in this book although God Forbid!! although why do I keep playing the football parley with my bookie ??

The above sample is that of a man of forty-three. He is a college graduate; however, he failed in medical school. As a boy he stuttered, and he was always self-conscious and often confused. The good form level of the script reveals that he is perceptive; yet, he has always had difficulty in expressing himself.

At the time this sample was written he had already abandoned his educational endeavors and become a carpet expert in a furniture store where he was relatively successful.

His script reveals the total insecurity of his personality, his extreme fear of being a failure. As he became more self-assured, he tried to meet his obligations, but was always handicapped in expressing himself freely. The neurotic fear of failure necessitated serious psychiatric attention.

This writer is a woman of sixty-nine. From the light and uneven pressure and the great irregularity of her script, we can gather that she is a highly dependent person. The personal pronoun "I," which is completely closed up, shows how much

Hi – Been here 3 months Now

Some nice days – mostly foul weather – they say

"it's – unusual" of the other day – snow, showers, Thunder

lightning & hale – rain?! all at once !!!! – with a line

Hope your well, well – yo better

c/o Hopel Westerner

est Stone & Broady

Tucson, Arizona

(See page 70)

she is involved in herself, and, in addition, there is a lack of stamina exhibited by the continually altering slant. One can surmise that this otherwise nice person will need constant psychiatric attention.

The sample on page 69 was written by a forty-seven-year-old man who had great mental and physical potential but never learned to utilize his abilities fully.

The handwriting is loose, irregular, and feeble. Almost all the letters are incomplete and intricate—a reflection of his distorted ego. He tried several different careers, but did not succeed at any of them.

His parents were divorced when he was eleven, he was deeply attached to his mother, whom he jealously guarded until she died when he was twenty-nine. The fact that his younger brother was highly successful made him feel particularly slighted, and he lost all will to try harder in his own field. His depression eventually became so aggravated that he required psychiatric treatment in a mental hospital.

Summary

In all these instances we find frustration of the drive to know mother love, or its logical substitute, producing anxiety and despair in addition to a long-term, unabated hunger for love which may finally find expression in a number of mental diseases.

There is undoubtedly a close relationship between psychic and physiological development. A child with psychological problems will often develop physical symptoms. Handwriting requires fine motor control, and, at the same time, it also reflects the state of the unconscious mind. Thus, it unites both physical and mental processes in the human being. The subtle alchemy whereby love is transmuted in the child into what is required for somatic, as well as psychic, development may, at the moment, be obscure. For this reason, it would be wise to have the handwriting of every youngster who has emotional difficulties analyzed. Through handwriting analysis the underlying problems can be discovered, and intelligent, competent treatments can be begun.

8. Cultural Aspects of Mental Illness and Psychotherapy

MODERN PSYCHOTHERAPY is rooted in two traditions of healing —the religious and the scientific. Modern healers combine the roles of priest and physician. Certain personal histories should be viewed as symbolic expressions of internal conflicts or as disturbed relationships to others or both. Often it can be assumed that the patient laid himself open to attacks by some weakness of character; therefore it seems likely that mental illness has its source in anxiety, despair, and similar dark emotions. The person may be in conflict within himself and out of harmony. Often sick thoughts can be replaced with spiritual enlightenment, and in such a case there is a good chance that the patient can be healed.

Psychiatric illnesses and psychotherapy are intimately inter-woven with their socio-cultural settings, and the illnesses are the result of or expression of disharmonies within a person and between him and his society. Because an individual's pattern in perceiving and relating to others reflects his internal psychic state and, in turn, affects it, these are two sides of the same coin. The cause-effect sequence runs both ways. A person's internal harmony or conflict affects his relationship with others, and his interpersonal experiences influence his internal state.

The distinction between the various types of healers and advisers lies less in what they achieve than in the persons with whom they achieve it. This, in turn, depends to a great extent on the setting in which they work. The very same patient might be treated by a psychiatrist, a psychologist, or, still yet, a clergyman. All three have formally recognized their area of common concern by forming the Agency of Religion and Mental Health. This chapter on psychotherapeutic practitioners would be seriously incomplete without mentioning the thousands of religious healers who have, in many cases, successfully treated the victims of mental illness.

This is the handwriting of a man of thirty-five, who is fairly wealthy, due to wise investments and knowing how to seize opportunities. He has inspired confidence and devotion in many people and once succeeded in borrowing money from friends by making up a story that his wife was pregnant and needed hospital care. Finally, when confronted with the facts he admitted that he had borrowed the money on a shabbily manufactured pretext. Nevertheless, he retained the lender's affection for a long time; although he never returned the money.

If, as in this case, such a person has an artistic personality, he may lead a full and successful life. His script is full of flourishes and exaggerated lower loops, revealing his eccentric behavior and the fact that he lives in a fantasy world, far removed from reality. His case history shows that he developed a bizarre and unrealistic way of living and eventualy became an alcoholic. Fortunately for him, he met a Christian Science practitioner who was able to put his life to rights in a Christ-like way. The man then overcame his alcoholism and grasped the essence of the doctrine of Christian Science. In this way he came to realize that his emotional problems were not unique, but were shared with others. His eyes were opened, and he became a useful member of human society.

Dominique and myself wish to thank you for your kind thought at Christmas time. Dominique, Christine

This writer, a man of thirty-six, has many normal mid-century attitudes, including a tendency toward suppression of his sexual urges and a strong compulsion to overwork as a defensive measure against his over-active sexual instinct. He is a cyclothymic individual, though apparently within "normal" limits. The blown-up lower loops and exaggerated capitals, in addition to the long initial strokes, reveal a person who has not found himself and is still influenced by unresolved problems of his youth.

He is intelligent and capable, but has never reached the place in life he desired and deserved. In an interview he mentioned that he was troubled by fear of himself, as though he might do himself injury or, indeed, go mad.

Psychoanalysis was suggested, and he responded freely. After many sessions he succeeded in ridding himself of the debilitating fear and began to respond to treatment in general.

This writer is a woman of forty. The extreme narrowness in so large a script as hers reveals that she suffers from anxiety neurosis. She is a talented dress designer; however, anxiety has crippled her ego and caused the usual fear-reaction—increased fibrillation of the heart and resultant tension. This eventually caused her to have a nervous breakdown.

Her illness originated when she was twelve years old and her father, who was then her only source or relief from tension, was killed in a street accident. Although she claimed to have no conscious recollection, there was a succession of sexual traumata, which left her mind in a state of complete confusion. Years of treatment, however, restored mental health so that she could, to a reasonable extent, function normally.

This woman's handwriting reveals that she is highly intelligent and imaginative. Her script is fluent, with original formation of letters, and, in addition, a good form level.

She is about thirty, lives always in a state of nervous tension, excitable, overly and negatively impressionable. This writer is, on the one hand, an interesting and animated talker and, on the other hand, filled with suspicions and fears, never really trusting anyone. Note the light, uneven pressure and the falling endings; the latter indicative of suicidal tendencies.

Despite her attractive personality, she is given often to empty, exaggerated accounts of her encounters with people. She freely allows her imagination to run away with itself. The fluency, in addition to the light pressure, discloses her innate meta-physical understanding. This was her greatest help in overcoming some of her negative qualities and in learning to live a constructive life.

Summary

The fabric of a harmonious personality is woven by a multitude of cultural factors. Consequently, there is no one simplistic solution to any personality disorder. The psychiatrist may make a contribution. So may the cleric. So may the psychologist, and so on. One professional may solve the riddle of mental instability, or indeed, it may require the coordinated efforts of both the priest and physician.

Conclusion

The last step in making a handwriting analysis is to perceive what is behind the letter and the script as a whole, thus behind life itself. It is the vision of the interpretor that shows the individual his way toward the light.

Clients are constantly coming to me and asking, "What is the meaning of my life?" It is not up to the graphologist to attempt to solve such problems. This question must be answered by each individual for himself. The graphologist who is confronted with such questions may well be driven into a corner, since his clients usually expect him to provide solutions for every type of problem.

Man lives in three dimensions: the somatic, the mental, and the spiritual. The last cannot and should not be ignored, for it is what makes us human. To be concerned about the meaning of life is not necessarily a sign of neurosis. One thing seems to be sure: the proper diagnosis can be made only by someone who can see the spiritual side of man.

Bibliography

Beers, Clifford W., *A Mind That Found Itself*. Doubleday, 1948.

Boehm, Werner, "The Role of Psychiatric Social Work in Mental Health," in *Mental Health and Mental Disorder*. Arnold Rose, ed. W. W. Norton, 1955.

Frankl, Viktor E., *Doctor and the Soul*. Alfred Knopf, 1955.

Jahoda, Marie, *Correct Concept of Positive Mental Health*. Basic Books, 1958.

Marcuse, Irene, *Applied Graphology*. Macoy Publishing, 1946.

———, *Guide to Personality Through Your Handwriting*. ARC Books Inc., 1965.

Maslow, A. H. and Mittelmann, B., *Principles of Abnormal Psychology*. Harper & Row, 1951.

May, Rollo, *Psychology and the Human Dilemma*. D. Van Nostrand Co., Inc., 1967.

Menninger, Karl, *Man Against Himself*. Harcourt, Brace & World, Inc., 1938.

Sonnemann, Ulrich, *Handwriting Analysis*. Grune & Stratton, 1950.

Storr, Anthony, *Integrity of the Personality*, Atheneum, 1961.